THE WONDERFUL WORLD OF
J. WESLEY SMITH

THE
Wonderful World of
J. WESLEY SMITH

By BURR SHAFER

AUTHOR OF *"Through History with J. Wesley Smith"*

THE VANGUARD PRESS, INC.

New York

"It seems that juvenile delinquency is on the increase."

"Mr. McCoy, I'm from the Great Northern Life Insurance Company. Your name was given to me by a Mr. Hatfield, who told me that you might be interested in a policy."

"Do you spell 'hunt' with one dog or two?"

"Don't be silly. Mr. Thoreau will be DELIGHTED to see us."

"Let me tell you about the dream I had last night, Dr. Freud!"

"SHOW me some of these atoms, Lucretius, and maybe I'll accept your theory."

"We like your manuscript, Count Tolstoy, but we just aren't interested in a war book at the moment."

"You mean you'd make me PAY to sleep here? Why, a fellow named Procrustes just offered to put me up free!"

"Monticello is a pretty name, Mr. Jefferson, and no doubt it's well constructed—
but the design! I think you ought to sue the architect."

"A new tub for soap-making . . . candle molds . . . a churn . . . wool carders . . .
You must just sit all day thinking up things for me to buy."

"And another thing. If all us Spartans are warriors, who'll pay the taxes?"

"But, Mr. Morse—giving up your art career just to play with dots and dashes?"

"It seems we are to go right ahead—and you should have heard what Admiral Farragut said about the torpedoes."

"It's a new unemployment project—Rameses calls it a pyramid."

"I want the design to be conservative—it should look like a
cave or a hollow tree."

"Oh, I'll print it all right, Mr. Paine—but a title like 'Common Sense' isn't
going to appeal to very many people."

BURR SHAFER

"As a preliminary step, I suppose, we might recognize them on a
sort of *de facto* basis."

"All I know is that guy named Guy Fawkes asked me to watch these barrels."

"So—on what big deal did you outsmart Baron Rothschild today?"

"So I said, 'Captain Bligh, we've put up with all we intend to
take from you' and then . . . "

"So that's the Mona Lisa! Well, Leonardo, old boy, it looks like Lisa del
Gioconda, all right, but you did something funny to the mouth."

"But, Cicero, I'm positive Catiline is just a harmless liberal."

"But I can't shoe your horse by tonight, Mr. Revere! I've got Lon Hasset's
team to do, and Squire Gordon's bay, and . . ."

"And see that this gargoyle is replaced immediately!"

"What a relief! It isn't a skull and crossbones, after all, Captain Smith!"

"My trouble is I'm forty thousand years ahead of my time."

"We're so proud of Wesley—he's found a way to take all the
wheat-germ out of flour."

"I've heard they're fixed."

"Let's row back to Norway. I couldn't stand another
of these Maine winters."

"I'm too old for any more helter-skelter stuff. I've settled down
here as Trotsky's assistant."

"But these ridiculous fairy stories, Aesop. Why not spend your time on serious
literary endeavor that will last?"

"Why don't you rewrite that part about the 'rocket's red glare,' Francis?
Rockets are practically obsolete."

"Fellow citizens! Are you tired of having to pay five cents for meat? Ten cents
for butter? Twelve cents a dozen for eggs? Then vote for . . . "

"Now, don't drink too much, Ponce. I don't know very much about the problems of teen-agers."

"How are yours on hills?"

"You heard me! Now, take me to your maharajah!"

"Why not just tell them Caesar committed suicide?"

"I'm sorry, Mr. Thoreau, but Mr. Walden says you can't fish in his pond."

"How was I to know such a pretty girl could be a witch?"

"Move from Egypt? But I've just begun to accumulate some seniority!"

"Dogs and monkeys will fly through the sky in machines that will strike terror into the hearts of men. Horseless carriages will grow bigger and bigger, then smaller and smaller. Women will paint their nails the color of blood, and the paint sellers will have a scandal that will rock the nation . . ."

"I was going to walk on just two hands. Then I decided to hell with it."

"Now to face Mrs. Smith. THIS is the moment of truth."

"I think Rome's economy is cracking up—all the empty lots are filled with chariots. Everywhere you go, you see used-chariot sales."

"But let's be fair about this—Attila has done a lot of good things, too."

"I'm afraid little Nero will never set the world on fire."

"And if you're not out by twelve o'clock, General Washington, I'll have to charge you for another day!"

"That Lady Godiva can't begin to ride a horse as well as I can."

"However, Your Majesty, don't think we cake bakers
don't appreciate the testimonial."

"I had no idea these Sabine women were so HEAVY!"

"It's utterly fantastic! Who ever heard of crossing a stream without getting your feet wet?"

"And your teeth are like pearls, I suspect . . . "

"Of all the colossal nerve! I let him borrow my cape, and look what
he does with it."

"Bread and circuses! Bread and circuses! What I want is Social Security."

"Ah, good morning, Mrs. Chippendale."

"There's only one solution—don't make buildings so tall."

"See here, young man. Why weren't you at fire-worship last week?"

"You can't bring that popcorn in here!"

"I've been hearing about this cotton gin of yours, Mr. Whitney—now, there's a drink I'd certainly like to taste."

"Mrs. O'Leary, your name has been selected as one of the citizens of Chicago entitled to buy a J. Wesley Smith patent non-spillable lantern at a special introductory price . . ."

"What's the name of that beanpole debating with Stephen Douglas?"

"It isn't the lack of representation that upsets me—it's the taxation."

"Why don't you do a story about me, Mr. Alger? How I inherited this business from my father and . . ."

"But, Monsieur Rousseau—if I go back to nature, how will I have money for any more of your pamphlets?"

"Be careful on these land grants. I've heard he's trying to stick you with New Jersey."

"I wonder if I could get the boys to plug this song I wrote."

"The grain didn't get through—but I brought you a new price administrator."

"That's all for today, stupid."

"Me tell that nosey paleface that Niagara River give him nice safe canoe ride
from Lake Erie to Lake Ontario."

"You're right—I picked out the wrong hunting ground, I'm too inexperienced
to lead—we need a new chief—I resign."

"Now that poor Count Cadillac has gone back to France, his name will soon
be forgotten in this Detroit wilderness."

"Will a skeleton key do?"

"If you'd take those rocks out of your mouth, Demosthenes, maybe I could understand what you're talking about."

"There stand the walls of Sparta, and, with one exception, every man is a brick."

"I happen to be thinking—whatever that is."

"Let me see—did Mr. Revere say, 'One if by land and two if by sea' or 'Two if by land and one if by sea'?"

"Maybe this'll teach you to watch how you change traffic lanes on the Appian Way."

"I don't know anything about Alaska, Mr. Seward, but the fact that the Russians are willing to part with it looks mighty suspicious."

"What a pity—a beautiful tower like that could have made Pisa famous."

"This is my last voyage! Maine needs a new industry and I'm going back to start canning sardines!"

"Most all-prevailing monarch, ruler of the universe, controller of all things, master of all fates and destinies, joy of . . ."

"I know it tastes funny—but think of how you'll be able to tax it."

"Why don't you physicians write prescriptions in Latin so
everyone can understand them?"

"Good heavens! This is terrible! It comes to three percent of my salary."

"Listen, Chaucer, if you want to go to Canterbury, GO to Canterbury, but stop asking me to go along. I've BEEN there, and it's a dull trip."

"Take it easy, Romulus. Athens wasn't built in a day, you know."

"I'll just call it *Brahms' Lullaby*. How do you like it?"

"Pyramids rise and fall. But what our next speaker has to say will
always be remembered as . ..."

"This business of taking from the rich and giving to the poor could
easily become a political theory."

"Aren't you afraid, Mrs. Ross, that thirteen stars will prove unlucky?"

"I'm going to Europe for six months. Don't sell any of my stock until I get back."

"And I can prove it by Baron Munchausen here!"

"Never mind the emperor—salute the press box."

"Sorry, Signor Michelangelo—the Sistine Chapel won't need a paint job for at least a year."

"Couldn't you make it a little fancier, Mr. Edison? We want something to sell on time payments."

"It's not that we're afraid, mind you—we just can't afford to
defeat any more countries."

"Another thing about buying this western territory—it'll be a good place to
have Presidential candidates from."

"Which one of you is Sitting Bull?"

"Other men catch bears and wolves, but all you ever get me is these little minks."

"I said, it's stuffy in here."

"A funny thing happened to me on the way over to the castle."

"Oh, that's just our water-boy, Gunga Din—you wouldn't find
him interesting, Mr. Kipling."

"Never mind the King's winery—we're supposed to be storming the Bastille."

"This new generation just hops around with no end in view—when I was young
we had war dances and rain dances and they made some sense."

"Up, man! Who ever heard of a seasick Viking?"

"I don't feel very insulted this morning, do you?"

"Welcome home, Wesley—tell me all about your trip with Ulysses."

"I'm leaving this place—every time I try to drill for water, some black stuff flows up."

"That, *Mon Empereur*, is the little village of Waterloo— a place of no importance."

"What your face should have launched is a bigger army!"

"There's no use getting mad, Mr. Tchaikovsky—all I said was that your new composition would make a swell popular tune."

"Instead of just sitting there reading Malthus—why don't
you help out around here?"

" '*Morituri te salutamus*'—whatever THAT means."

"Don't take chances—call the humane society people."

"Another thing, General Washington, if you were the first President, you wouldn't be able to say you inherited your problems from somebody else."

"Anyone for discus throwing?"

"Remember, men—they attacked us first!"

"It's all set, boys—just one more speech by some fellow named Bryan, and then our candidate gets the nomination."

"I'm sorry I ever suggested health food to Nebuchadnezzar."

"V—IV—III—II—I—oh, for the love of Mars!"

"Surprise! I've traded in all this old furniture
by Chippendale for modern Victorian."

"We've just discovered Vinland!"

"No! No! I meant throw the OTHER rascals out!"

"It's called money. The government either gives it to you or takes it away."

"98 . . . 99 . . . 100."

"Frankly, Mr. Stuart, you're in a rut."

"Oh, you think so, do you? Would you care to step out
in the cloister and say that?"

"I don't like to box with the Marquis of Queensbury—he keeps making up his own rules."

"I wonder why Damocles moved my place card to the center of the table."

"The old girl's daft! She told me that someday John D's grandson would increase my taxes!"

"But this is all wrong — I'M the sheriff and YOU'RE the cattle rustlers!"

"I was Chaucer's secretary—but I got fired because I couldn't spell."

"Something's wrong with our laddie. He's still awake and I've been playing a lullaby for a solid hour."

"But would they remember ten? Maybe you should give
them two or three at a time."

"Half a league, half a league, half a league—Mr. Tennyson, can't
you come to the point?"

"Stop making promises—you're already elected."

"That will be five years—with ten days added because of the change-over
to the Gregorian calendar."

"All well and good, Mr. Edison—but in a typical small town who's going to volunteer to stay up all night generating electricity?"

"It is unthinkable that the citizens of Rhode Island should ever surrender their sovereignty to some central authority located way off in Philadelphia."

"Instead of this return trip to the new world—why don't we just raid Paris again?"

"A vacation? You mean you actually want me to pay you for three days when you won't even be here?"

"I won't collect any more rent from Franz Mesmer, I won't collect any
more rent from Franz Mesmer . . ."

"I simply cannot accustom myself to the tempo of modern travel. To think that
I left London only two months ago and here I am in New York."

"You can stick here in this dinky village if you want to, Herr Kant, but I intend to travel and make something of myself."

"I STILL think that retort I gave Oliver Cromwell was rather clever."

"It's a new-fangled thing the boss bought—I'm quitting Saturday."

"You should have heard the denunciation I had prepared for Nero—if
only I hadn't fainted."

"I doubt if a runt like you, Bonaparte, has any qualifications for leadership—
but I'm giving you a try as acting corporal."

"First or second round?"

"I never could lick these Roman numerals. How much is XXVI plus CLXXIV?"

"I'm afraid we'll have to go back to bronze. This new stuff rusts."

"Happy birthday, sweetheart—I bought you a mummy case."

"It'll never work. People will go blind looking for the right key."

"History will NOT ignore Your Majesty—you forget about Louis XV furniture."

"Try to remember. Was it an oak tree you put the charter in?"

"What puzzles me is how a fellow like you could make so much
not to pay taxes on."

"I've finally perfected my invention. All you have to do is pull it."

"Haven't you any others? This sheet is printed crooked and
the word 'Postage' is misspelled."

"No, no, Samson—apply equal pressure, like this."

"I could dig up some hot stuff from his past if I were
sure he wouldn't retaliate."

"This new calendar—how will it affect charge accounts?"

"And while I am not actively seeking leadership of the tribe, I would take it if offered."

"Nothing like these foreign jobs—only half the upkeep."

"Not on Maiden Lane! You'll have to take them over to Broadway!"

"Do you mind if I go to lunch early, Professor Pavlov?
For some reason I'm hungry."

"We'll never get anywhere by creating law. If people are going to eat each other,
they'll eat each other, that's all."

"Of course, we're only sending up monkeys now, but it won't be long until you see Wesley up there."

"I know I predicted fair and warmer—but let me explain about the sudden appearance of this low-pressure area . . ."

"I'm sorry, Noah, but I have my depositors to think of, and a loan on
an ark just doesn't seem . . . "

"Oh, your price for the land is most generous. But, frankly, we were looking
for a somewhat better class of customer."

"His name is J. Wesley Smith and he's wanted in Manitoba."

"And so you want to be admired as a brave hunter, but at the same time you're
afraid of tigers. That's why your stomach hurts."

"Never mind why—we're moving to Florence and changing the name of the firm."

"And just how did you get in Frederick's Potsdam Guards?"

"Forget about Plato and his ideas and listen to me."

"Now, listen again. 'Honored judges, most noble lords,
your most gracious majesty . . .'"

"Don't bother to outline a program—just criticize the previous administration."

"Oh, Washington himself is all right. It's the men around him like
Jefferson and Adams and . . ."

"I don't like it. It's against nature."

"I'm sorry, Mr. Poe, but you know very well you can't keep a pet in your room."

"Suppose we go into orbit."

"If you ever tasted one of Ellen's wheat-germ loaves, King Alfred, you wouldn't feel so bad about burning it."

"I'm a revenue officer, and a revenue officer is supposed to—oh, never mind."

"Go ahead and nominate anybody you want—I can't stand tobacco smoke."

"Herr Beethoven says that he is too deaf to hear your new composition, and to thank you for reminding him that his affliction is not always a handicap."

"I see the Dodgers defeating the Yankees in the World Series
—whatever that means."

"And remember on that last Crusade how those oriental
spices upset your stomach."

"I may not be able to hit anything—but this is ONE shot that's going to make
a lot of noise."

"I think people will understand you better, Mr. President,
if you just say 'eighty-seven years.'"

"But, Galileo—why should you study moon craters when right here at home
most people don't have satisfactory bathrooms yet?"

"Find out who's behind this vicious sabotage. Someone in the paint department
has deliberately put two different colors on this motor car."

"Lucky for you, Sir Walter, that I was on hand when that thing caught fire."

"Your cooking is always the same. At the Borgias', things have fascinating new tastes."

"I think, Mr. Fahrenheit, that most people know when it's hot or cold enough to take off their coat or light a fire."

"I feel out of place in this outfit—I'm a vegetarian."

"But I'm NOT Dr. Livingston—go away!"

"And for the final joust of this tournament, the challenge is accepted by our last remaining knight—Wesley Coeur de Poulet."

"You'll have to get rid of this junk, Professor Volta. I just touched something and got a terrible shock."

"Take him first. He was our public relations man."

"Then it's agreed — we stop fighting, and the taxpayers support BOTH
the king and the nobles."

"Sure, I voted to ostracize Aristides. Now, how do you spell J. Wesley Smith?"

"It's intolerable, General Washington. The farmers of Valley Forge deserve more consideration. Drilling at all hours, drums scaring the livestock, and several chickens stolen. We have friends in the Continental Congress, you know . . ."

"Now, my idea, Your Majesty, is a stamp tax for the American colonies—
it will be painless and easy to collect."

"So much for tigers. Now, suppose we try domesticating reindeer."

"Of course the world is flat—but he's so cute."

"Well, we've lived through this terrible first winter. Now, to clear some ground,
take our seed corn, and . . ."

"Well, then, if I can't help—is there anything I should tell Mrs. Horatius?"

"The defendant hasn't a chance. He's engaged some green lawyer from
New Hampshire by the name of Webster."

"It seems he saved money for quite an elaborate tomb. However, the taxes were raised last year and . . ."

"That unruly young Andy Jackson came into the bank today and paid off his loan."

"A fine Minute Man YOU are—we've been waiting half an hour!"

"Your time is valuable, Mata Hari. Hereafter devote yourself to someone who can remember a troop movement if he sees one."

"I'm in a hurry to get home so I'll go with Ulysses."

"Go away! Christmas was over two days ago!"

"I just wanted to make a musical out of *Pygmalion!*"

"Another reason you better come in on our side—French is a harder language
to learn than English is."

"Now that we're at peace again, let's hang the couriers we used for
all those insulting notes."

"But I hate kings! I went to the palace to bore from within."

"A wrist watch? I'd as soon wear a petticoat!"

"Every time we conquer a country now, we make them citizens. In no time a Roman will have no more status than an ordinary human being!"

"Good heavens—building right on top of us! What's to become
of Coney Island at this rate?"

"My brother has an idea that we should grow beards
and manufacture cough drops."

"We've just discovered California—this is the first release
from their publicity department!"

"Another thing we don't like about it, Mrs. Stowe, it
wouldn't sell in the South."

"—and this is final, Herr Bach. Either you stop this silly composing and spend
more time rehearsing the choir boys, or we get a new organist."

"Oh, Jefferson is a good man—but I'm not sure I like the idea
of a civilian being President."

"Mr. Hippocrates, I wonder if you can help my nephew get into medical school."

"It's a new story by that Dickens fellow—about a worthy banker named Scrooge who finally degenerates into a sentimental weakling."

"About this 'Liberty or Death' business, Mr. Henry. Isn't there some
reasonable position in between?"

"You tell Adam Smith that I might accept this manuscript if he would put in
a few amusing anecdotes here and there."

"But, Diogenes, this is ridiculous—you could qualify for
the new public-housing project."

"Mr. Dick Turpin here has kindly consented to act as my escort—I'm a little
worried about carrying all this money."

"Stop calling me Willie Shakesberg, and don't ask me 'What's in a name?'"

"When Mr. Carnegie brought me from Scotland I thought he wanted
me to perform in his famous hall."

"And another thing, Mr. Clemens, I want you to stop these feeble attempts at humor you have been sneaking into your copy."

"Whenever I think of you, it makes me want to write something where the lines end with the same sound."

"To tell the truth, Mr. Franklin, we merchants would like a little less about thrift and more about spending."

"It's about your boy James, Mr. Watt. He was over my house playing with a teakettle full of boiling water, and when I remonstrated . . ."

"Certainly we can find a better governess than that mousy little Miss Brontë."

"Why don't we just nominate the Governor of New York—
whoever he is—and go home?"

"Wesley went over to have a peace talk with the chief of the Narragansets."

"No, I didn't commit any crime—they just gave me an aptitude test."

"Did it occur to you, Captain Kidd, that you and I will be the only ones to know where this treasure is hidden?"

"But, General Hannibal—we're out of peanuts!"

"You go on to California, get a good job, and send for me."

"I've got a better idea—we'll rob from the rich and keep it ourselves."